NATIONAL GEOGRAPHIC

T0288463

River of Life

PATHFINDER EDITION

By Karen Ross and Elizabeth Sengel

CONTENTS

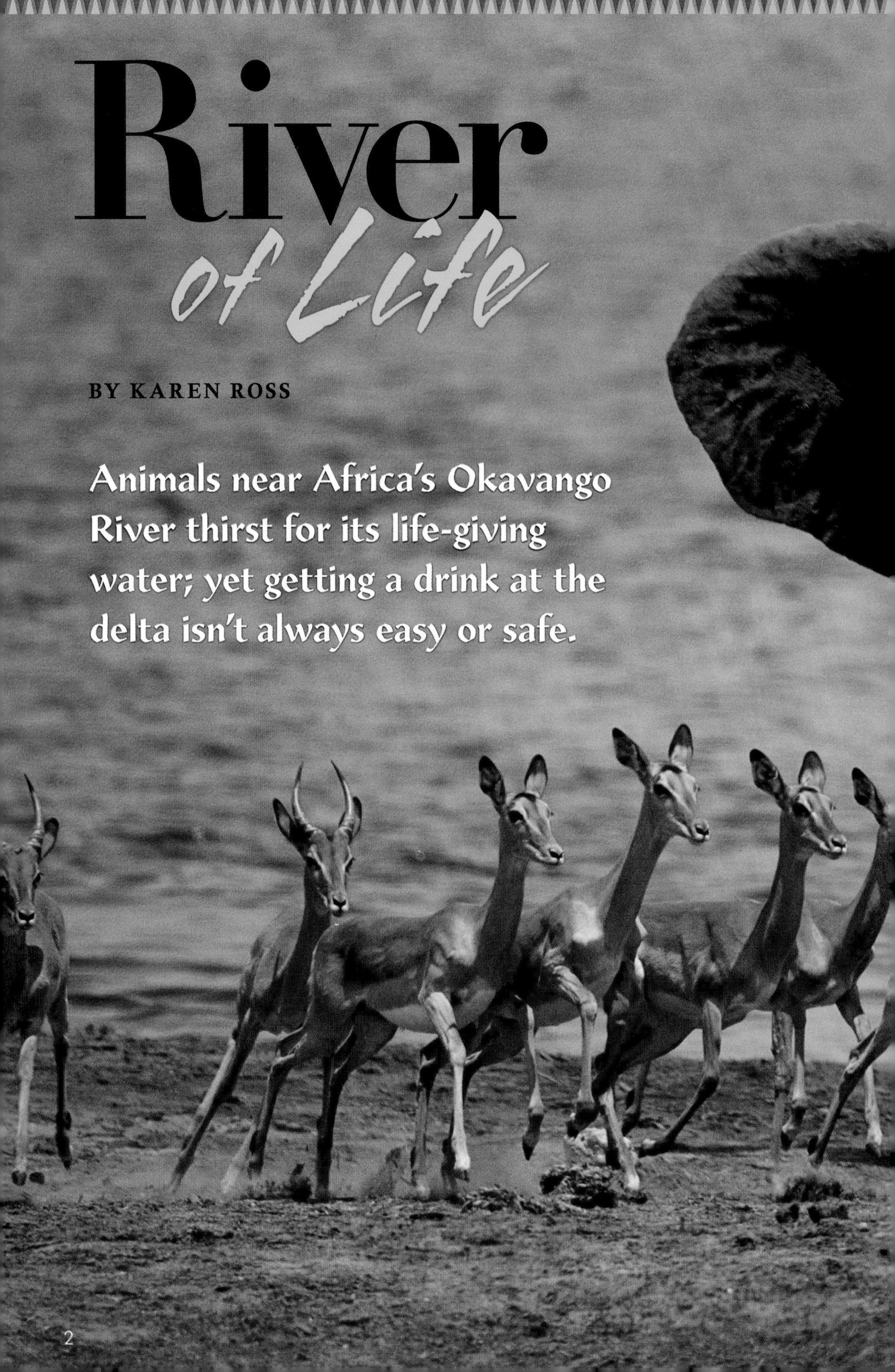

River of Life

BY KAREN ROSS

Animals near Africa's Okavango River thirst for its life-giving water; yet getting a drink at the delta isn't always easy or safe.

Meeting Place. *Creatures great and small come together to drink from the Okavango River.*

What's the most valuable thing in the world? The answer to that question may depend on where you live. Here in the Kalahari Desert, water is more valuable than just about anything else. The desert is in Botswana, a country in Africa. Not much rain falls here, so people depend on the Okavango River for water.

This river, which starts out as rainwater far away, flows for nearly 1,600 kilometers (1,000 miles) before ending in the desert. As the river ends, it spreads out, forming a wide **delta**. The delta provides food and water to the people and animals that live nearby.

The delta is a great place to meet the animals that inhabit the area. After all, they have to come here to find food and shade from the blazing sun.

On the River

One of the best ways to meet the people and animals that live here is to float down the Okavango River. That's why I am sitting on a pile of soft grass in a small canoe called a *mokoro*. My guides and I will explore the delta.

Batsilewa and a few of his friends, who were born and raised here, are my guides. They are members of a group called the baYei people. Batsilewa uses a wooden pole to push our boat down the river. We glide through beautiful water lilies.

I soon spot several small animals living near and on the water. Small birds sparkle like jewels against the river water, and tiny reed frogs hide in the water lily flowers. Then I hear a haunting cry above. I look up and spot what made the sound—a large African fish eagle.

I watch as the eagle soars through the sky. Suddenly, it plunges downward toward the water, stretches out its sharp talons, and uses them to pluck a fish from the water. The eagle then flaps its way back into the sky.

Termite Islands

Next we pass tiny islands, where many kinds of fruit trees thrive. From the *mokoro*, I notice berries and figs, and we stop at an island for a break. I sit in the shade of a palm tree and snack on its sweet brown fruit.

Sitting on one of the delta's small islands, I think about how it formed. Insects called termites built each of the islands during the dry season while the area was dry. Then the river flooded the area again. You see, termites build large **mounds**, and the tallest mounds peek above the water. Tree seeds landed on the mounds, the seeds sprouted, and eventually trees covered the islands.

Water World. *The life of local people is focused on the river, which provides them with almost everything they need.*

Above the Okavango Delta

Hundreds of islands dot the Okavango Delta. The maps show the delta during the wet and the dry seasons. How does the area change?

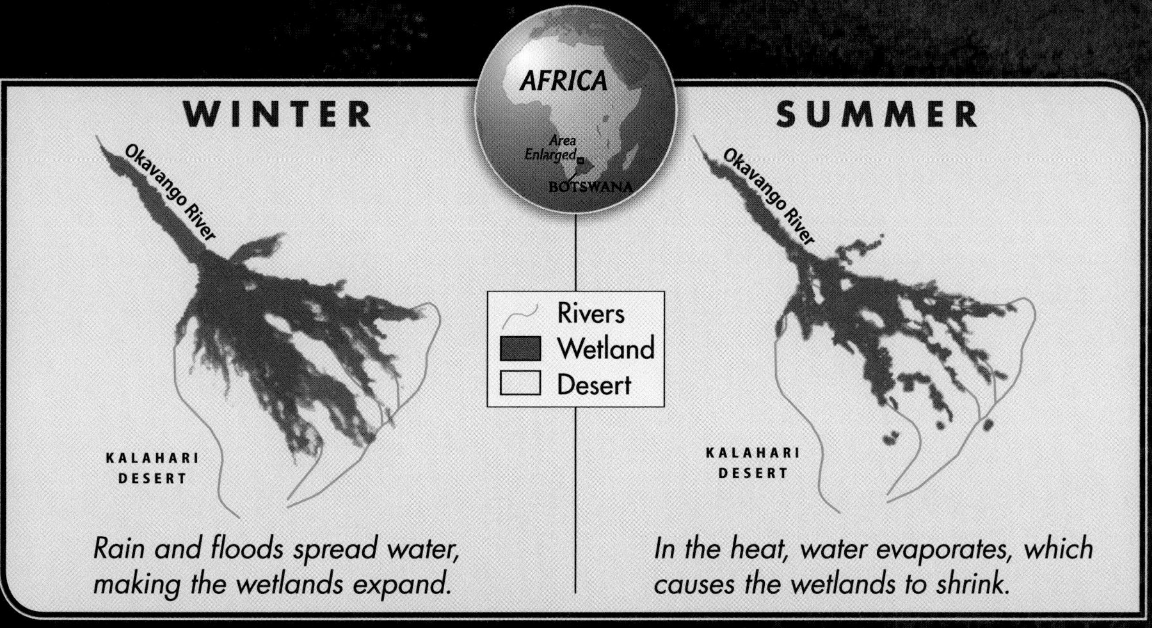

Rain and floods spread water, making the wetlands expand.

In the heat, water evaporates, which causes the wetlands to shrink.

Meet the BaYei

I finish eating my fruit snack and hop back into the canoe. As we head south through the islands, I enjoy listening to the baYei guides, whose speech is musical. I ask Batsilewa what village life is like.

He tells me the delta provides all people need. Take baskets, for example, which everyone uses. Baskets are used to serve, store, and carry just about everything. Women weave beautiful baskets from palm leaves that grow nearby. Some of the basket designs are called "tears of a giraffe" and "knees of a turtle."

The baYei consume lots of fish, and nearly everyone helps with the fishing! Men use nets to catch fish, but women use a different method. They place baskets, which look like long funnels, underwater. Then the older children chase fish into the baskets. Babies watch all the action from baskets strapped on their mothers' backs.

Predator and Prey

As I listen to the guides, we pass the last of the termite islands and begin to observe herds of large mammals.

I spot zebras grazing on grass. Buffalo cool off in the river, and red lechwe, a kind of antelope, dance across the shallow water. We surprise another kind of antelope, the sitatunga, which leaps from its reedy hiding place. Impalas are everywhere.

Everything seems peaceful, but it isn't. All kinds of cats—big and small—also come here, and they are ravenous.

Lions, leopards, and cheetahs act like they own the river. Small wild cats called servals and caracals sneak around quietly. They need to eat, too, but they are smaller, and they don't want to get eaten.

Next I spot a pack of African wild dogs, which is an **endangered** species. Most live here in the delta. A dog pack works together to hunt prey. By hunting together, the small dogs can attack much larger animals. They have to eat fast because lions and other large predators are always on the lookout for a free meal.

A Lion's Roar

Suddenly, I hear a lion roar. A lion's roar can be heard eight kilometers (five miles) away, but this one is closer—much closer. As I swivel toward the sound, I see a strange sight. A pride of lions is in the water; the adults are wading while the cute little cubs bob and swim.

You may think that most cats hate to get wet, and you're correct. These lions must be very hungry. Even these big, tough cats must work to get a meal. The animals are crossing the river to find prey, but the wet lions do not look happy.

Lions hunt many of the animals that live along the river. Sometimes they can find a free meal, but often they try to steal animals that other predators have hunted and killed.

What's for dinner? *This lion hopes to catch a buffalo for supper. Lions are fierce predators on the delta.*

Gone Fishing. *These women will use their funnel-shaped baskets to catch fish.*

King of the River

People sometimes say that lions are "kings of the jungle." This is not true at the delta, where elephants rule.

Elephants are not only the largest land animals, but they are also the second tallest animals. Only giraffes are taller. An adult male elephant stands about 3.4 meters (11 feet) at the shoulder and can weigh 5,400 kilograms (12,000 pounds).

Elephants are famous for their large ears and trunks. Each ear can grow to be more than a meter (3 feet) wide, and their trunks can carry up to 270 kilograms (600 pounds).

Elephants don't eat meat; instead, they munch on grass, water plants, and fruit trees. To get food, they can use their heads as battering rams. An elephant knocks over a tree, which allows it to easily reach the tender leaves at the top.

Predators can't hurt these towering adults; however, they can attack young ones. So the adults have to watch out for their young. Hungry lions are not afraid of a baby elephant.

Luckily, it doesn't take much to scare off a lion. A protective elephant can scare lions away with a stomp of its foot.

Looking for Water

I see elephants of all sizes at the water's edge. Adults drink and rest, while younger ones play. Many swim. They are everywhere. Botswana has the largest elephant population on Earth, with about 100,000 pachyderms, or elephants, living here.

Elephants are fun to watch, but they're also important to the delta's **ecosystem**. During dry months, the desert swallows the delta, and much of the river's water dries up, making it harder for people and animals to find water.

That's where the elephants come in. It's up to them to find and then dig up water from underground streams. After the elephants drink their fill, the other thirsty animals drink the leftover water. This system works out well.

Delta Dangers

Life at the Okavango Delta is always hard. Sometimes there's too much water, but at other times, there isn't enough. Just getting water can be difficult. Hungry animals are always looking to hunt smaller or weaker animals. So it can be dangerous for them to search for water.

Yet smaller animals make their way to the water because they must. They need water to **survive**. Watching them, I realize the importance of water and wetlands, or areas where water and land meet. For the animals and people of the Okavango, a wetland is home. Without it, life would be impossible here.

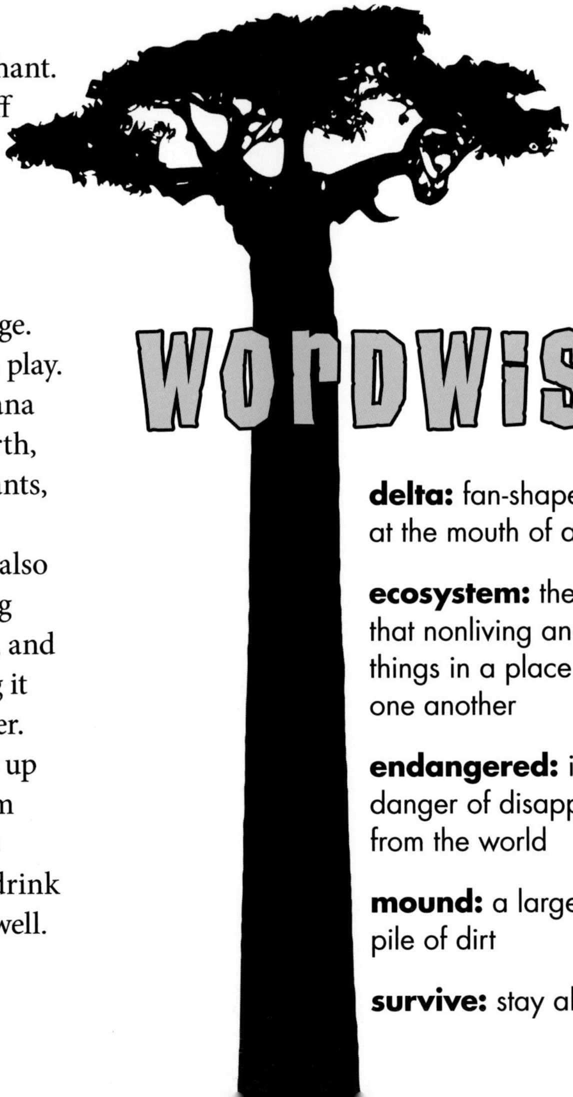

WORDWISE

delta: fan-shaped area at the mouth of a river

ecosystem: the way that nonliving and living things in a place affect one another

endangered: in danger of disappearing from the world

mound: a large round pile of dirt

survive: stay alive

Big Boss. *Forget lions. Elephants are really in charge at the delta.*

Water Fun. *A hippo passes the day by playing in the river.*

A Day in the Delta

By Elizabeth Sengel

Elephants

A group of adult elephants and calves come to the edge of the river to drink water.

Hippopotamus and Fish Eagle

A fish eagle uses the broad back of a hippopotamus as a perch. Hippos spend their days grazing on river plants. They smash vegetation when they walk, creating new channels where water can flow.

The fish eagle swoops low over the river to snatch a meal!

Crocodile

A crocodile exhibits aggressive behavior as it emerges from the water. People in the delta fear these large reptiles.

Lions

A young lioness looks into the camera. It follows other lions as they cross the river.

Cheetah

At the end of the day, a cheetah stations itself at the top of a termite mound. The mound provides a good lookout point for surveying territory.

Delta Days

Follow the river to answer these questions about the Okavango Delta.

1. How do islands form in the delta? How do trees reach the islands?
2. What things does the river provide for the baYei people?
3. Why do elephants rule the Okavango Delta?
4. How do different kinds of animals use the Okavango River?
5. Why is the Okavango a river of life?